Apologies that never came

Also by Pierre Alex Jeanty

To the Women I Once Loved
Her
Her Vol. 2
Him

Apologies that never came

Pierre Alex Jeanty

Andrews McMeel Publishing
a division of Andrews McMeel Universal
1130 Walnut Street, Kansas City, Missouri 64106

www.andrewsmcmeel.com

23 24 25 26 27 VEP 11 10 9 8 7

ISBN: 978-1-5248-5064-7

Library of Congress Control Number: 2019931040

Cover Design: Celia James
Editors: Carla DuPont and Patty Rice
Designer/Art Director: Spencer Williams
Production Editor: Amy Strassner
Production Manager: Carol Coe

This is for the ones looking for closure,
the ones trying to make sense of it all,
the ones trapped in their mind and courting sadness.

This is for the ones running with heavy feet after healing,
the ones who are doing everything to find their smile,
the ones who will not let finding love be a dream that dies.

I am sorry that they didn't turn out to
be what the beats of your heart were
looking to tune in to.
I'm sorry that they weren't the cup of
tea that could soothe your soul.

Oh, regret

Here it comes to reclaim your soul once again, fighting to seize your thoughts and make you a slave to bitterness, again.

Here it is assaulting your joy, with a knife to the throat of your happiness.

Here it is confirming your doubts, reminding you how many times *"I love you"* has been used as bullets fired by the voices of smooth criminals who disguised themselves as lovers.

Here it comes,
here comes regret working its spell.

Visitor

Love has become a season,
one that comes right after spring and
leaves right before the fall.

Right when your heart began to smile
and your guard began to sink.

Right when your fears began to hide
themselves and courage began to slowly
stick its head out to breathe in fresh air.

Right when you were putting your
heartbreaks behind you and allowing
yourself to fall into the hands of new
experiences.

Right when you began to believe that it
was here to stay . . . it leaves to its next
appointment.

I was blind

You slowly became the embodiment of
"ignorance is bliss."
You chose to ignore what was in front of
you so it did not cut in between the dance
we were having with happiness,
or scratch the love song playing between
the two of you.

Like the eyes ignore the nose though it's
right in front of them, you turned a blind
eye to their true color so it did not bleed
itself into the pure connection you
believed was breathing between the two
of you.

You stayed blind until your eyes eventually
became red from the countless red flags
that pulled tears out of them.

Then you threw the white flag,
surrendering because there was nothing
left to ignore.

You were different

Their mouth carried truths that your heart fetched like no other,
truth that was not only planted on their tongue, but grew roots that grabbed onto your heart.

They were everything you needed them to be and everything you wanted in love.

They were the angel you were glad lost their wings and became a citizen of this earth.

How could you have guessed that they were one of the fallen ones who visit the earth to mimic everything love is?

Most of us don't know what liars, manipulators, or cheaters look like; only those who cast judgment put a face to those characteristics.

Role-play

You never saw yourself being a character in another short story.
You played the role again, falling in love with the hero only to find out the plot twist was that they were the villain who perfected the meaning of "*wolf in sheep's clothing*."

You played the "*don't judge a book by its cover*" role only to realize that you should not have done so, because the summary was far too exciting to be truly heavenly.

You were right.

Here you are, expecting long chapters of a lasting story, only to become the lasting moment of another short thrill.

Enough

I am sick and tired
of being both sick and tired of these empty
promises that have given my stomach
reason to reject any food that tries to
make its way in.

I vomited lie after lie
and became dehydrated from this thirst
for you.
You could not quench it, nor were you
willing to give me more than sips of your
love.

I am sick and tired of being the one who
got away when I had every intention of
staying.

I have become sick of this word "love," but
never too tired to give up on my quest for
it.

Stuck

The way they held on to their ways was the
way you wanted them to hold you.

The way they kept breaking their promises
was the way you wanted them to keep you
smiling.

The way they kept running away from your
love was the way you wanted them to
chase after your heart,
over and over and over again.

Unfortunate it is that they stuck to their
ways, instead of sticking with you.

Frustrating it is, but those ways made way
for you to see your way out.

Got me

They had you convinced that they were
praying for something good,
but they were only preying on someone
good.
They were looking for someone good
enough to convince that they, too, were
good enough for a loving relationship.

They had you convinced that their heart
had been stomped on as well, and that
they too were afraid to take the next step.

Yet they became the one you had to be
afraid of, walking all over your heart in
their thick rubber boots, stomping on
every bit of love growing.

They had you convinced that love was
what they were starved of when they were
full of empty promises and false hope.

They had you convinced . . .

True religion

Their words were sermons you found easy
to commit to,
words of life that gave your heart courage
to beat again.

Their lips became a bible.
In their eyes, you saw a savior willing to
forgive your sinful past and grace you with
their love.

Loving them became your religion.
Faithfulness like theirs could only be found
in radicals, so you grew to believe that
they would sacrifice their very flesh for
your heart.

Monday came,
and servicing your heart became a charity
instead of devotion.
Slowly, they resurrected the ugly things
you'd known,
allowing you the realization of the truth
that all this happened as a conquest to get
into your pants.

Foolish thinking

You're not a fool for being fooled.
Almost everyone will pour sugar into their
food if it's placed into a salt container.

Until they taste it, they will not realize what
they've done wrong.
Almost all of us have met someone who
has "forever" in their eyes and "happily
ever after" written on their skin;
yet, they only came for a short stay.

Maybe?

Perhaps they were different,
and the ending was the only similarity to
the others.
Besides, with this thing called love,
you either find your forever, or you find
another stepping-stone for the path.

Maybe you're lucky for meeting new faces,
catapulting you to new places, though they
never remain the face
that you wake up to every morning.

Not so different

Love will not send you someone *"so different."*
They will be dressed in flesh,
you will draw unto each other like magnets,
they will whisper similar promises,
you will have to find reasons to trust one another,
they will tell you truths that resemble the lies you've heard before,
you will fall fast,
they will undress their heart,
and you will pour yourself into them.

The difference is that the right one will outlast the days. The truths will stay as truth,
the lies will come with sincere apologies and true repentance,
and the fall will be one you won't need to get up from.

"I regret meeting them. I wish I never fell for them."

Such words will echo in your thoughts when heartbreak strikes. It's almost second nature for us to wish we never had any part of bringing pain to our own doorsteps. We wish we could go back and change our decisions.
Unfortunately, we can't. We can only live above them.

Regret will always show its face when we are hurt, but it will never heal a thing. It will never create a better path, but it will encourage us to remain stuck in the past to dwell. There are things in this life you cannot control; you can only control how you rise and grow from it.

Grow from your failures.

I am sorry that they misled you to
believe that their love was destined to
be, ruining what you'd been waiting
on from the hands of destiny.

Disappointed

Disappointment hangs itself around your
neck, slowly tightening its grip,
like those albino snakes that people love
taking pictures with for show.
For a split second, the photos make some
of them appear to have their feet on the
neck of their fears. In reality, their fear is
only filtered out for likes.

They slithered into your life, slowly choking
every doubt out of you, awakening in you a
love that swallowed your fear of being hurt
again.
Then they blindsided you, leaving new
scars on your back with their venomous
teeth.

How is that possible, you wonder,
that they made you feel so fearless only to
give you more fears?

Well played

There was a certain peace in having an
empty phone, a safety in knowing that
your heart wasn't at risk
because it was on the sideline watching
others play this game of love.

But then an invite came.
Out of nowhere they found you, and you
found reasons to drop your walls to
entertain the idea of giving out your
number.

You played the numbers game, which is to
pique their interest and see if they could
keep yours.
You played the texting game, looking to
see what game they would play because
you have been through enough of them to
recognize them by name.

Fast-forward, here you are in love, and
your game did not recognize theirs.
You never saw yourself becoming another
number in their numbers game.

Is theirs real?

Couples showing teeth and wearing love
used to warm your heart.
It doesn’t now,
and winter has found your heart in an
alley, homeless and bruised.

You were once a couple in love,
not only once, but not even too long ago.
You were once a couple with them,
smiling without reason,
talking about the silliest things,
laughter never leaving your lips,
and kisses always coming at the right time.

You were once feeling the touch of love,
but now its name sounds like Hitler;
its voice sounds like knives,
its face looks like a genocide.

Seeing people dressed in it only makes you
sick.
Hoping this ends sooner than later.

Not only

It's not only the words they once said that are haunting you,
it is the words they never said;
the words that you were hoping found a home in their mouth,
words you wanted their voice to carry to your ears.

It's not just who they once were to you
that keeps confusion barking at you,
but also their slowly fading potential
and their break in a different direction
when they weren't too far from the finish line.

It's not only them who you are holding on to, but everything that could've been.

Transformed

My skin became vacant with you,
an abandoned building that I visited during
the days that being with you kept doubt in
my mind.
I molded myself into the spitting image of
what you preferred,
laying my identity at your altar as a
sacrifice for love.

But you changed your preference and
found more reasons why my true colors
weren't painting what your eyes desired.

I became what I thought you'd love, only
for you to tell me that a love for me didn't
have a home in your heart.

Afraid of letting go

While these hands of mine worked to grab
onto our future, yours lost their grip on me
as you tried to hold on to your past.
You hugged tightly the truth of your bad
experiences and the lies of your fears,
giving them power to distort our current
reality.

While these hands held on with the hope
that you would wake up and see that I was
fading out of your life,
you closed your eyes, meditating on the
lies of your ego and drowning what we
had.

In being afraid of letting the past go, you
let me fall into your past.

Free will

You are not responsible for how another creature uses their free will.
You find it troublesome to control even yours at times.
So, when you choose to blame yourself for what they chose,
you have to realize that there's another choice that exists.
The choice not to.
It was the same option that tapped on their shoulder and reminded them that they could choose to end something good, or not.
Yet they chose it.
They chose it by themselves.
But you carry the blame like a curse, like hurting you is a burden that you should carry for your betrayer.

It is rare to find someone guilty of the crimes that have been committed unto them.

Right thing

There is only wrong in making a god out of
humans who are just like you.
Believing in love and staying faithful to
who you thought they were
can never be sin.
Doing right to the wrong people can never
be wrong.

Games

We all fell for magic tricks and believed in things that weren't real.
Wrong turns are part of every journey and U-turns are always allowed.
We've all been the laughing stock, but the joke doesn't have to last forever.
The pain isn't immortal, its days are numbered as well.
Tomorrow will eventually come stumbling with love in its hands, ready to give to you a love that will not have contradicting faces behind the mask.

"I am disappointed at how things ended more than anything, hurt by who they've turned out to be."

We've all been fooled by something or someone. We've seen things go a different direction than expected. It happens when we expect the person we are loving to do their part and love us the same, yet they don't. When it happens, it hurts. No one goes through this life without meeting some type of hurt or pain. Do not let that disappointment lead to a disappointed life. Do not let it harden you heart, do not let this failed attempt at love, despite what number of try it is, make you give up.

It's okay to be disappointed. It's frustrating when you play the fool, but it's not okay to give birth to the fear of disappointment that will rob you of a life of love and loving life.

I am sorry that they awoke a flame in
you that they weren't ready to feed.
I am sorry that they've helped you find
the worst in you.
I am sorry that it's becoming harder to
find the best in you.

Empty airports

Them being unprepared and unready for
love was never your weight to carry,
but you packed their fears of love
and red flags with your baggage.

You convinced yourself to play hero,
willing to fly wherever it took for the
relationship to find its heaven.

But they crashed,
shutting down over and over,
damaging your wings.
Both hearts couldn't be united
and the arrival of love delayed again.

Burning

There goes anger,
watching you walk with disappointment all
over your face, catcalling you using the
worst language possible.

There you go,
slowly being lured into listening to the
spellbinding words of resentment.
Your speech slowly evolved from "*Why did
this happen to me?*" to "*I'm so freaking
stupid for falling for this dumb crap again!*"

There goes anger, convincing you to let
this fire burn bright instead of putting it
out, refusing to let it find a way to burn
good things from you.

There goes anger,
joining regret to do a better job at
overtaking your soul and making a bed out
of misery for you to lie in.

There you go.
Hope it goes.

Preparation

How could you not see that I was willing to give every part of me for the smallest part of you?

How could you not see that a hunger for me in your eyes was all I ever wanted?

Did you not see a future in our future as well?

Innocent

How do they get away with committing such wrong?

How does piercing someone's heart, walking away, and leaving them to drown in their blood not count as attempted murder?

How does someone find it easy to live life smiling after having hurt the soul of someone who only offered them love?

Our justice system has found it hard to rightfully condemn even the guilty at times; the innocent-until-proven-guilty policy has had a say in this.

How could they believe they were guilty when they claimed to have innocently invaded your heart with the attempt of loving you, a task which became something they couldn't do?

Guilt has a way of confronting people and pulling confessions out of their lips. Unfortunately, it won't happen to them. Their intent never wavered, only their words and their actions.

Ironic

A thief robs with a cause in mind;
they take what they want without caring
whether you may need it more than them.

There are old lovers who are greater
thieves, robbing people of their pure love
and hearts full of good intentions, only to
put them on a plate of bragging rights for
their egos to feast on.

What is the point
of sacrificing someone's belief in the very
thing that causes us to be alive, for the
sake of doing what makes you feel less
dead inside?

The irony is that the very thing they are
taking from others is the very thing that
will truly make them feel less dead.

Rivers

Blurred vision,
teary eyes,
pain turned liquid,
mourning someone who isn't worth a
thought.

Crawling down your cheeks,
your eyes keep on raining.
Thoughts clouded by memories that
should've never been made.

Bottle of emotions popped open,
poured onto shoulders of friends
who remind you of all the reasons not
to . . . but you can't help what's felt.

Fiery

Everyone who has been a victim
will feel the rage.
It is those who become victors who learn
to let the rage feel them,
becoming its lord and repurposing it.

X-Files

You thought this universe hunted down
and captured another being from another
planet for you to love, for the species here
didn't know how to be kind to your heart
and loving to your soul.

Here they were, finding something
magnificent in your smile, mesmerized by
your thoughts, fascinated by your
existence.

Here, they treated you as if you were more
than human and barely less than GOD.

Here, they disconnected from their
previous life and perfectly synched
themselves into yours.

Then their exes slowly found their ways
into this love story, becoming a bother,
weeds that found their way to grow in the
middle of green grass.

There stood their ex, begging them to
come back to the other planet where they
had a different life, living with different
motives.
There settled their ex, slowly pulling them
into a vacuum they seemed to find
comfort in.

There went their promises, being washed away like words written on beach sand. There they went, being pulled into their old life, leaving that new thing to grow old and stale.

There they went, being just another person who said their ex was a terrible excuse of a person, using the same mouth they used to spit terrible excuses about why they made their way back.

Venting

Your once-innocent tongue has become a cemetery that only hosts a tombstone with their name.

This is how you bury who they once were to you:
you dig deep enough,
throw their name into the hole, then
throw all the dirt they've done into it.
Your friends' ears become witnesses to these secrets, exposed to the flaws you'd forced your eyes to miss for love.

It makes you feel good to speak of the bad they came packaged with.
"*They weren't all that anyway!*" your friends scream, giving you comfort while you agree with them. And it's not because you care for the truth in those words, but because this is your therapy and you have to let it out.

Slipped up

You caught me slipping and I fell right into
your arms,
sucked right into your life and leaving mine
behind.
I found new friends and new reasons to
keep old friends in the past for you.

You caught me slipping,
stumbling out of old hurt and right into
new ones.

You caught me slipping, and this is why
anger swells my lungs and my breathing
becomes as inconsistent as you were.

Falls like this hurt, but I know once I get
back on my own two feet, my knees won't
grow this weak again for strong words
from weak characters.

"I freaking hate them. It makes me angry that they played with my heart."

In every stage of breakups, anger will find us. If not controlled, which it often isn't, it will inspire decisions that will lead to terrible choices with all variations of consequences. You wouldn't be human if you didn't have a moment where you grew mad for being madly in love with someone who now acts as if what you both built was nothing.
You wouldn't be human if the pain didn't enrage you, knowing that if your eyes would've been wider, you could've dodged it altogether.
Listen to me: staying angry only makes you miserable. It hurts you and transforms you.
Get angry, but force it to leave. Cool off eventually. It happened to me, it happened to others, and it's not terrible luck that led to this.

I'm sorry that you had to carry this
pain; you had to fight not to let it take
the health of your mind
or steal your joy.
I'm sorry you had to fight to remain
true to yourself and true to love.

Depressing feelings

As the thought of them eats up your days
and nights,
depression slowly crawls,
smelling and scratching,
moving like a dog finding the perfect
position to lie.
It circles and digs,
like the dog looking for his treat in
quicksand.
It is sniffing out the best place to bury itself
underneath your skin, into your mind,
to give you a reason to fall in love with
being numb and being broken.

Broken

They say, *"Just get over it,"* while they themselves hold on to the silliest habits that have found homes inside of the fiber of their existence.
Therefore, they refuse to accept the eviction and are unwilling to obey without force.
See, people love to tell you to let go when it isn't the same thing they are holding on to.
They love to give advice for the situation they don't struggle with, only to ignore their own struggle.
In their struggle, they do the same; they cuddle with the pain, justify the reason it is still there, then take however long possible to close the door on it.

Forgive to forget

Here you are once again, trying to take back the episodes of a show that far too many eyes have seen.
Embarrassment cripples your fingers as you rush to scroll through images that are no longer part of a bigger picture.
Your face is booked tonight, your eyes busy trying to find photos of the two of you in each other's presence and bury them into a past that is hidden.
Maybe it will help them forget that you are struggling too.

You're at it again, asking yourself when you will meet someone who can stay in the picture, someone who won't be cropped out later, someone you won't waste your "likes" on.

Here you are, doing what it takes to forget when the forgiveness has yet to come.

Unfortunately

This pain, it aches deep.
To take off your armor and lay it at the feet
of someone who you hold dear,
only for them to create a losing war for
you is brutal.

To strip your soul naked and only find
interest in stripping clothes from your
body is a different type of cruelty.

It is unfortunate, but this is life. There will
be people who prefer money over what it
can't buy,
who prefer that cheap Dollar Tree glitter
over gold,
and the physical over what can't last
beyond lustful moments.

Trapped

You're stuck in bed, dark curtains hugging
the window space made through the wall.
The blinds sometimes allow light in, but
that's why this curtain is here.
You don't want any light to find its way
inside your room before it finds its way
inside your heart.
The tears make their way back again,
your eyes are puffy again,
throat dry again,
the memories are being replayed while
everything pauses for you a-g-a-i-n.

Your mind can't find its way out of feeling
fooled, while your heart can't find the
words to speak on anything besides the
pain.

You are trapped again.
They say misery loves company, so maybe
that's why you feel this weighing you down
mentally, physically, and emotionally.
This sadness is here to conquer every part
of you.

Unfair

You wrestle with the idea that all your labor
will become the harvest for someone else.

Rightfully so.

How do you labor hours in a garden only to
be told that the home it added life to will
no longer be yours?

How do you put all your eggs in a basket
only to be told that this basket belongs to
someone else, and the broken eggs are the
only things that are yours to keep?

It is a heavy burden to prepare yourself for
forever with someone who is only here for
now.
It is being robbed for what you fought to
be yours.

Unfortunately, you can't fight in the ring
alone.

RIP X

You saw them as a caterpillar
who would one day wake up with the sun
smiling at them and wings sprouting off of
their back.
On that day, they would see that they
were a butterfly whose home was made of
flowers, with freedom to stretch across the
sky.

You saw change knock on the door of their
soul, waiting on the other side like a
salesman playing his convincing game.
But the process did not show up,
and their potential was not the package
being delivered.
Instead, it was damaged goods at your
front door once again.
They changed to become a moth larva
feeding you blanket statements about
love.

Now here you are, trying to understand
the changes, trying to make sense of it all.

*The unfortunate thing is that not every
existing caterpillar becomes a butterfly.*

The other side

Why couldn't it be you who they are
smiling with, taking out on new dates,
dishing out all the efforts for, and putting
their hearts on the plate for?

Maybe they are only pretending to serve
this new love their all.
Maybe it's all a show like it was with you,
and behind the curtains is mess.

Maybe they are hurting worse, just doing a
better job at trying to move on than you.
Maybe they aren't even happy; maybe it's
Instagram and this love is just a filter
enhancing the reality others see.

Perspective

Cloudy days are nothing to love unless
you've known the loneliness that will try to
swallow you through dark nights.
Pain is nothing bad if you have never had
the good that is the opposite of it.
Water will never be "needed" if you have
never met dehydration and never known
what it means to be thirsty.
How would you have known what love
isn't, if you've never met people who could
offer it to you?

WYD

You are not a poet,
yet you have mastered the art of wearing
your heart on your sleeve, hoping it would
become their favorite shirt.

You pour your feelings drip by drip into
text messages like poets pour ink on to
paper.

You write things you wish they knew,
things they should know,
things you want them to care for,
although it is only wishful thinking.

You let your words sit still. Hesitant you
become, staring at the send button as if it
were a door into the place right before
hell.

Well, that's because it is.

Forgive you

Forgiving yourself is the thing you're supposed to do when you make a mistake that leaves lasting impact.

Being unable to catch yourself from falling for someone who did everything right to sweep you off your feet is not a mistake.

It is all rather a choice that cannot be erased, but can be repurposed to become lessons that teach you what to fall for next time.
It can show you how to let yourself slowly down into it, instead of allowing your heart to drop you into them.

Summer always shows up

Your existence is now baggage you're
becoming convinced isn't worth carrying.
There's so much bad packed in it.
In every pocket you find either pain,
sadness, or bad luck.

You believe that the end of the pain is
ending yourself.

Oh no, the pain doesn't end when you end,
the pain is meant to be lived through, and
it is meant to be crossed as you find your
way into healing.

Ending you will only give other people a
pain to carry and cross themselves.

Heartbreaks hurt, but nothing hurts more
than death, though you are not around to
feel it.

You must believe this is just a season.
Mother Earth has proven far too many
times that seasons change and some are
easier to enjoy than others.

"I don't know how to be anything but sad; depression is taking me. Since it all ended, I only know how to be sad nowadays."

There are phases in our lives that will drag us down. Heartbreaks take a toll on all of us. Many of us lose our appetite, and lose our desire to do anything; we lose our smile and our strength. The bad is not that it's happening, the bad is staying in it and allowing it to destroy you. Those who find beauty in this life are those who stick around and cross the rivers of sadness.
The light on the other side will seem like a myth, but those words have been proven to be true countless times.

I've been through heartbreaks myself; either I did the heartbreaking or I was the one heartbroken. Now, I am happily married with a beautiful family and a future I never imagined when I was mourning the loss of my ex.

The burden gets lighter and eventually it'll fall off your shoulders.

I am sorry that you had to let go when
all you wanted to do was hold on.
I am sorry that you had to sprint
forward, leaving what you thought
would always be behind you.

Better leave when *"better"* leaves

I was hoping that the *"better you"* found us before I left to find a *"better me."*

I was hoping that we could've started a new chapter before the book became ashes from a fire you made to keep your cold heart warm.

I was hoping that the end never came, but the loving lover I waited for missed their bus.

Let go and let God

They say to let God cut in and give Him the
burden to carry from here on out.
My God,
don't they know that the burden to carry
is everything you have left of them?
It may be unhealthy, but it is the only thing
remaining since they left.
You pray, asking God to give you a sign
that they weren't the one, while the
relationship stands as a monument for
your answer.

Addicted

This addiction is killing you;
you've stopped injecting yourself with their promises, but the residue of false hope keeps you wondering if they'll fulfill any of them.
People keep telling you to put them in the past, but here you are, yearning for their presence.
Out of rehab you've gained the strength to never show your face in a text thread with them again. Now, you do not know how to handle their calls or see them physically.
There's a gravitational pull to them, a weakness that hid itself behind your newfound strength.
You are more than aware that they are everything bad for you, but like fast food, they satisfy your taste buds.
Giving in has become more convenient than letting go.

Heart vs. mind

Here we go again.
Bodies of memories stretch out on the
floor, bloodstains cover the field,
a civil war is taking place again
over nothing that should be fought about
at this point.
Your heart and mind have become siblings
fighting over toys,
over how the game should be played.
Your heart argues that you must follow it
because it knows love.
Your mind interrupts and says that this is
"hurt" because it has been through
enough to know.
"You know nothing but walls of defense!"
screams the heart.
*"It is better than being naive and
welcoming imposters who come to destroy
this temple,"* replies the mind.

The war continues . . .

Doing better without you

The gym has become your favorite home,
and shedding calories has become better
than shedding tears.
The latter makes you look ugly, while the
other one makes you look better than
before, unearthing the jealousy in their
heart.

You can't wait for them to see how your
body has changed and how you are looking
way better than before;
it is the perfect disguise for your
unchanged mind and the fact that things
aren't really getting better.
You wish their eyes would drool when they
see you and that they would want you
back,
but you know it is their mouth that will
become watery and their hands that will
beg to grab hold of your skin once again.
Physically, it'll provoke them, but mentally,
it will be another loss on your end.

Undependable

Your fist is clamped as tight as can be.
Your hands are bleeding and your
stubbornness tells you to hang on,
to go without a fight,
but this isn't a fight;
it is self-hurt,
it is stirring a pot of self-inflicted pain.

Where is the good that was supposed to
come of this?
Where are they when loneliness is beating
every inch of hope out of you?
Where are they when you are drained
from emptying your eyes of tears?
Where are they?
Not here.
They haven't been here to cup your face,
sacrifice their shoulders, and let you know
everything is going to be okay.

Time

You hear that time heals all wounds, but
your clock seems to have the seconds
mixed with the hours and the hours with
the months.
The days come like molasses dripping,
the minutes like a snail traveling.

You hear that time heals all wounds, but it
feels like it's on vacation and your turn
won't come for another century.

Here you are, waiting for the healing to
come and work an overnight shift on you.
It never came, and you are realizing that
it's not the days that end pain, it is what
we pour into those days that patches the
wounds and heals us over time.

What's next

Here is the fear, welcoming itself into your thoughts.
It has reason to, because it did not utter a lie when it said not to fall in love with them.
Maybe it was right about the person, but it was never right about love.

It is definitely not right this time.
It is tying your hands together to keep you from catching your next blessings.
It's trying to clog your thoughts with doubts so you make no room for better.

The beauty in letting go is finding freedom and making yourself available for more.

"What if I am closing the door on a good thing? What if they finally come around to be what I want? What if I never find anyone to replace them?"

The fear of being alone is real. The honest thing about it is it's not picky at all. It doesn't discriminate, it goes after everyone. Everyone who has tried being in love has faced it. Letting go would be an easy thing if we weren't so afraid of losing what we had despite how we may have been treated. We would rather hold on to something half-good than leave our hands empty. We have treated letting go as if it's taking a risk, uncertain of the possibility that something better is ahead. In many situations, taking a step out is something good despite what it may seem.

Separating yourself from what you know will always be hard and changing will always be challenging; but on more than enough occasions, it'll be the best choice you ever make. Accept that it will take time.

I am sorry that some wait until you are
gone to love you.
I am sorry that their apologies never
came when you needed them.

Cleanup

Here they are, running back as if they are walking on eggshells, carefully choosing their words, strategically texting their compliments, and doing everything they should've done in the beginning.

Here they are, tiptoeing around the broken pieces of your heart as if amnesia has washed their mind and they are clueless as to who made this mess of your heart.

Here they are, wanting you to welcome them back with open arms after they closed theirs when you needed to be held and cared for.

Maybe they need a reminder.

Tug-of-war

I pull back, you slowly draw me in.
Once I am in, you slowly pull back.
You are playing cat and mouse,
and I am trying to hold on to water.

Missing you

They wait until your love for them goes missing to start missing what they missed in the first place.

Here comes the devil asking you to be his again after you finally walked out of hell and dipped your toes into the air of heaven.

Healing comes with many beautiful things, but on its path are planted ugly things disguised as blessings that you've always prayed for.

There's no greater trap to keep you from moving forward.

Last laugh

Isn't it funny how you don't become what they can't live without until you are living without them?

You become oxygen to their lungs when you finally allow yourself to get some fresh air.

You become everything they missed out on when you are done missing them and nothing in you wants to resurrect that.

You become everything they need when you've found every reason to no longer want them.

Reminiscing

The thought of me being with someone else eats away at your happiness, spoon by spoon.

As for me, the thought of me being spoon-fed so many lies while believing you respected me enough to pour me some truth is what makes me sick to my stomach.

What I miss

I do not miss you anymore.
I do not even miss the memories; they no longer visit me to replay the better days of us while denying the bad ones that were bad enough to tear us apart.

I do not miss the embraces that carried empty smiles and naive laughs.

I do not miss your presence anymore because your absence has become far more fulfilling.

All I miss is the time I lost investing in you and chasing after you.

Two-player mode

You moved on in a heartbeat.
I moved on because I know why my heart beats.
See, I've learned that happiness can exist without your existence.

You flirted with those you said could never hold your heart and searched for a future lover.
I flirted with my potential, tasted some things I thought could never be mine, and fell in love with my future self.

The perfect tomorrow

The better days will come.
They will trail with heavy feet,
at the pace of elephants traveling.
Their flights will be delayed,
and they will come and go before they
stay.
But they will come,
and they will stay longer than before.

Those days will be yours sooner than later.

"They won't leave me alone now that I am done with them. I don't understand."

Humans tend to want what they can't have, only to no longer want it once they have it. Unfortunately, this is also something they do with other human beings' hearts. They will take you for granted when they should cherish you, yet try to cherish you when you are gone.
They will come and try to love you when the love for them no longer exists.

You are guilty of nothing but choosing what is best for you. Don't fall into that trap; second chances do not work more often than not. If nothing has changed, it will be a waste of time.

Be wise and protect all you've worked hard to become. Terrible pasts aren't meant to be relived.

I'm sorry it took you so long to come
back to yourself.
I'm sorry you've been kept away from
your strength for this long.

Oh, healing

Here it is, happily reuniting with you.
Here it is, begging you to make yourself at
home and get comfortable.

Forever it seemed to be since you were
caged under the dominance of heartbreak.
Forever it seems since you escaped.

Therapy

Every stroke of my pen is either about you
or about us.
It is not my way of holding on,
this is me letting go.
This is the draft of me writing my own
happy ending.
This is me documenting my story,
writing our end.
It's the beginning of an evolved me that
will never bow down to your perfectly
crafted lies and cry for another chance.

Affirmation

They say you are smiling more,
you tell them it is because you are taking
more care of yourself.

They say you look stronger,
you say it is because the past couldn't
swallow you
and you are being present in your present.

They say you look better,
you say that it is because your heart has
found reason to smile and is feeling free.

They say you look happy,
you say it took awhile to realize that you
are.

Who they are now

They have become neither a memory nor regret.

They have become a true reminder that love doesn't grow in every ground that you'll plant your heart in.

They have become the motivation to no longer pour yourself into people that are not only empty, but always with an open end only for receiving.

They've become the reminder to see love before you hear it and even then, to move cautiously.

Smiling

There you go, wearing a smile more often, dressing yourself up with confidence and laughter on your feet.

There you go, appreciating what you've been through because what it taught you cannot be learned in school.

Here you are, enjoying your freedom from the pain, your divorce from the heartbreak.

Here you are, being you and loving you.

Low tolerance

Now here you are:
you've developed a taste for better,
a hunger for meaningful relationships,
a true thirst for substance.
You've learned the voice of your intuition
and together, you are building a low
tolerance for things of no value.
You've grown allergic to time robbers,
closing the door quickly on
uncommunicative people;
people with tongues heavy with empty
promises,
leeches,
overly materialistic souls that can't afford
what you have to give.

Deserving

And now you see that the process was
nothing more than a lie.
You now see what everyone else saw:
a door of escape that lead to the oceans.

There was always better waiting on you.
You were always lovable,
you were always worth it,
you were always the perfect cup of tea.

Happy for you

This happiness that you've found without
them, hold on to it.
Nourish it, care for it, do not let anyone
steal it from you.
For in it there is peace; loneliness will
sometimes be on the prowl, but it will
never conquer.

This happiness is one that some don't find
because their feet became too heavy to
chase any longer.

This happiness that you've found, hold on
to it like your existence depends on it.

"I can't believe it took me this long to be done with it all. Now I am free, happy. I don't need them anymore."

When you finally get back to being the person you were before them and even better, you won't understand why you were stuck. I know you won't look back now, and all I can say is you've made it. You've overcome the unavoidable, you've overcome something that destroys souls and ends some lives.
There is always light on the other side if we keep walking. You found it. Please do not give anyone the power to take it ever again. If there comes a breach and they manage to capture it again, try not to take as long in claiming it back.
Congratulations, and be proud that you overcame.

Dear Woman,

I am sorry that there are men who are trapped in the flesh of immature boys who only act like men to make you fall for them, yet act like boys when it's time to catch you.

I am sorry that there are men who see your rejection as throwing their ego to a pool of piranhas. They respond with such hatred simply because you aren't interested.

I am sorry for the men you've crossed who only know how to express anger as an emotion; men who only show love when death shows its face.

I am sorry for the men who can't take your concrete, meaningful, "No," said in all seriousness, seriously. Instead, they see a dare, another goal to attain.

I am sorry for the men who invited themselves into your life without your permission, exercising power to rob what wasn't theirs.

I am sorry for the cowards who used their fists to disagree with a woman to get their anger across.

I am sorry for the men who said, "*I love you,*" with tongues of cactuses; men who promised forever with goodbyes ready to be summoned shortly after.

I am sorry for the men who are commitment-phobes, yet trying to suck everything good out of a woman.

I am sorry for the men who didn't know how to be good friends, good boyfriends, or good husbands.

I am sorry for the men who leave you empty, leeches who only drain the best out of you.

Dear Man,

I am sorry for the women with beautiful faces and ugly hearts who have served your heart the worst meal.

I am sorry for the women who misled you only to find themselves on the path of settling.

I am sorry for the women who use love as a debit card and treat your emotions as a losing war.

I am sorry for the women who assassinated your dreams and tied your legs with false compliments, encouraging your doubts to be stronger.

I am sorry for the ungrateful women who want you to chase things they don't need just for the sake of having it.

I am sorry for the women who convince others that they are victims, yet victimize you every chance they get.

I am sorry for the women who do not give you a fair chance at being a man to them simply because few men have been men to them.

Closure is not something that comes easily, it is something you chase and fight to have.
It is not a phase, but a thing that will bring back the happiness you thought they'd left with.
It is the thing that will always remind you that you are still a winner as long as you are breathing, despite the losses you've faced.

The beautiful thing about closure,
is that it's something you can gift yourself with;
you don't have to wait on what they need to do and know they won't do.

What are you waiting on?

If their apology never came,

here it is . . .

I AM SORRY.